Our environment

FACT FINDERS

Protecting our wildlife

Terry Jennings

Oxford University Press

Oxford University Press, Great Clarendon Street, Oxford OX2 6DP

Oxford   New York
Athens   Auckland   Bangkok   Bogotá   Buenos Aires   Calcutta   Cape Town   Chennai
Dar es Salaam   Delhi   Florence   Hong Kong   Istanbul   Karachi   Kuala Lumpur
Madrid   Melbourne   Mexico City   Mumbai   Nairobi   Paris   São Paulo   Singapore
Taipei   Tokyo   Toronto   Warsaw

and associated companies in Berlin   Ibadan

Oxford is a trademark of Oxford University Press

First published by Oxford University Press 1995
Reprinted 1998 (twice)

A CIP record for this book is available from the British Library

ISBN 0 19 916710 9

Available in packs
Our environment pack (one of each title)
ISBN 0 19 916706 0
Our environment class pack (six of each title)
ISBN 0 19 916707 9
Teacher's Guide 2 ISBN 0 19 916802 4

Acknowledgements

Illustrated by: Peter Lawrence (pages 4, 12, top, 13, bottom, 17, 21); Sara Woodward (pages
8–9, 11, 12–13, 18, 19, 20, 25, 26, 27, 28, 30)

The Publisher would like to thank the following for permission to reproduce photographs: ICI
(page 6, inset); Frank Lane Picture Agency (page 24, bottom left); Andrew Lawson (page 9);
Oxford Scientific Films/G I Bernard (page 24, bottom right); Oxford Scientific Films/Terry
Button (page 5, top left); Oxford Scientific Films/Michael Leach (page 26, inset); Still
Pictures/Mark Edwards (page 23, top); Wildlife Matters/Dr David Feltwell (page 11, bottom
right); Wildlife Matters (pages 6, main, 7, 23, bottom)

Front cover illustrations: Terry Jennings (background, bottom inset); Peter Lawrence (top inset)
Back cover illustration: Peter Lawrence

All other photographs are by Terry Jennings

With special thanks to Martin Race for agreeing to be photographed

Edited by Anne Priestley

Printed and bound in Hong Kong

Contents

Wildlife in danger

There are many different kinds of plants and animals in the world. But there are not as many kinds as there used to be.

Extinct plants and animals

Some kinds of plants and animals are no longer found. They have all died out. They are extinct.

◀ Dodo

▶ European cave bear

▼ Large blue butterfly

▲ Woolly rhinoceros

Rare plants and animals

Some British plants and animals have become extinct.
Many others are rare. Only a few of them are left.

Even some common plants and animals could be in
danger. We can all do something to help save our
wild plants and animals. This book shows you
some of the things you can do to help.

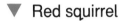 Red squirrel

◀ Camberwell beauty butterfly

◀ Otter

Bee orchid ▶

▼ Natterjack toad

▲ Corn marigold

5

The dangers

Some animals and plants are in danger because of chemicals. Waste chemicals from factories kill plants, insects, and fish. So do some chemicals used on farms.

Sewage
Some animals and plants are poisoned when sewage is put into rivers and the sea.

Losing a home

Many more animals and plants lose their homes when land is cleared for building new roads, houses, shops, and factories. Ponds and ditches are also filled in to make new land for building and farms. There is then nowhere for the water animals and plants to live, and so they die.

Make a wild flower garden

Many wild flowers are becoming rare. You can set aside a small corner of your school playing field for wild flowers. Or you can plant some wild flowers in tubs or pots.

What to do

1 Buy a packet of wild flower seeds.

2 Clear a patch of ground and dig it over. Break up the earth so you have an area of fine, weed-free soil.

3 Sprinkle the seeds on to it in the spring or summer. Cover them with a very thin layer of soil.

4 Do not let the seeds or seedlings dry out. Water them if the weather is dry.

5 Look at the different kinds of flowers that grow from your seeds. Insects and other animals will visit the flowers.

▶ Prince Charles planted large parts of his garden with wild flowers.

Make a butterfly garden

Butterflies feed on nectar. Nectar is the sweet juice that comes from flowers.

Nectar flowers
Some flowers have lots of nectar. If you grow them in a garden, or in large flower pots, butterflies will come to them.

Planting stinging nettles

Several kinds of butterflies have caterpillars which eat nettle leaves. The caterpillars grow and one day turn into butterflies. You could plant some nettles in a large pot of soil. The nettles will not spread because they are in the pot.

Butterfly eggs

Wear gloves and carefully look underneath the nettle leaves each day. Can you see any butterfly eggs? These will soon hatch into caterpillars.

buddleia

michaelmas daisy

marigold

ice plant

These plants are easy to grow and they have lots of nectar.

Rearing caterpillars

If you find a caterpillar on a nettle or other plant, you can watch it grow. You can see what it turns into. It may be a butterfly or a moth.

What to do

Make a home for your caterpillar from a plastic sweet jar. The pictures show you how.

1 Carefully put the caterpillar on the plant.

2 Most caterpillars eat only one kind of plant. Give the caterpillar new pieces of the same kind of plant you found it on every day.

3 Before long the caterpillar will turn into a chrysalis. It may first burrow into the soil.

4 Keep the chrysalis in a cool place. Check it every few days. When the butterfly or moth hatches out, let it go in the garden.

Swallowtail butterflies

Swallowtail butterflies are very rare. They are found only in one small part of Norfolk. Swallowtail caterpillars feed on the leaves of the milk parsley plant.

Wicken Fen

Once swallowtails were found at Wicken Fen. This nature reserve is in Cambridgeshire. But swallowtails died out at Wicken Fen in about 1950.

Rearing swallowtails

Some scientists collected a few swallowtail eggs from Norfolk. They put the eggs in large cages, with milk parsley plants. When the caterpillars hatched they fed on the milk parsley plants. They grew into butterflies.

Swallowtails at Wicken Fen again

In 1993 the first swallowtails were set free on Wicken Fen. If they survive and lay eggs there will be swallowtail butterflies at Wicken Fen again.

▲ Milk parsley

The bird garden in summer

In summer, birds need water for drinking and bathing. In spring and early summer they also need materials to make their nests. You can help the birds to find water and nesting materials.

Make a bird bath

Fill a shallow dish or old dustbin lid with water. Stand it away from places where cats may hide. Put clean water in the bird bath each day. Watch the birds come to drink and bathe.

Nesting materials

Collect different things birds might like to build their nests with. The picture will give you some ideas. Hang these up in a net bag.

wool

hay

hair

moss

feathers

Take care!

If there are birds nesting in your garden, do not go too near to them. The birds may fly away and leave their eggs or babies to die. And never take birds' eggs.

The bird garden in winter

In winter the cold weather makes it much harder for birds to find food. You can make a bird feeder and put food in it for the birds.

A bird feeder

You can make a bird feeder from an old vegetable tray. Ask an adult to put a screw eye in each corner. Tie your bird feeder to a branch of a tree. Put food in it for the birds. Brush the feeder clean at the end of each day.

Bird pudding

Ask an adult to help you make a pudding for the birds.
Fix a piece of string through the bottom of a clean
yoghurt pot. Stir currants, seeds, and breadcrumbs into
some melted fat. Pour the mixture into the pot and let the
pudding set hard. Then hang it up for the birds.

The birds still need to drink and bathe in winter. Give
them a dish of clean water every day.

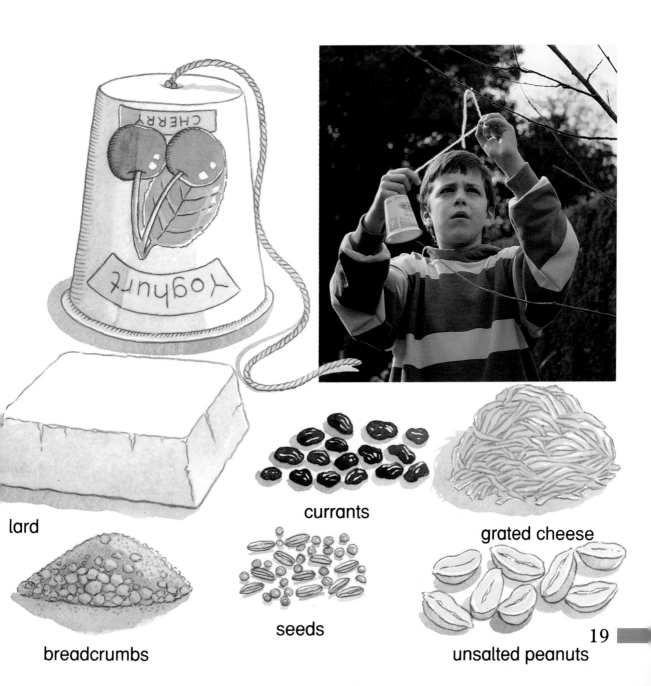

lard

currants

grated cheese

breadcrumbs

seeds

unsalted peanuts

19

Make a compost heap

A compost heap is home to all kinds of wildlife.

What to do

Collect grass cuttings and dead leaves. Ask for vegetable peelings from the kitchen. Pile up this waste material in layers. Put thin layers of soil in between. The pictures show you how. Leave the heap to rot for several months.

grass cuttings   dead leaves

vegetable peelings

Breaking down the waste

Small animals, and plants called fungi, help to break
down the waste material.

Animals

The inside of the heap gets very warm. That is why
voles and other animals like to nest there. In some places
slow-worms spend the winter in compost heaps.

In spring, spread your compost on the soil. It will help
garden plants to grow better.

Plant a tree

Trees provide food and shelter for wildlife. A large oak tree, for example, may be home to more than 300 different kinds of insects. You could plant a tree of your own.

What to do

In the autumn, look for some acorns on the ground. Choose ones which are just beginning to grow. Plant them in little pots of compost.

Keep your acorns well watered. After a few weeks, each acorn will send up leaves. When they get bigger, replant them in larger pots.

In the spring, plant your little oak trees in the garden or school grounds.

The Channel Tunnel

When the Channel Tunnel was built, a large oak wood was cut down. But first some young people collected acorns from it. They planted the acorns in pots. Later they planted the young oak trees near the Channel Tunnel.

Ivy

Ivy is a good plant for wildlife. During the spring, birds nest among its thick green leaves. In the autumn, butterflies and other insects come to feed from ivy flowers. Many insects and other small animals spend the winter under an ivy plant.

▲ During the winter, ivy has green berries. Birds come to eat these.

Growing ivy plants

Ivy plants are easy to grow.

1 Break off some leafy shoots about 10 centimetres long.
2 Stand the shoots in jars of cold water.
3 Soon the pieces of ivy will start to grow roots.
4 When the roots are 2 or 3 centimetres long, put the little
   ivy plants in pots of compost.
5 When the plants are larger you can replant them to
   grow against a wall or fence.

Nest boxes for small animals

Bats

Bats catch and eat a lot of insects at night. Most bats live in hollow trees and caves. There are not many hollow trees and caves now, and some bats live in old buildings.

Bat boxes

Some people help bats to find a home. They put up special boxes for the bats to live in. You can see two in the picture.

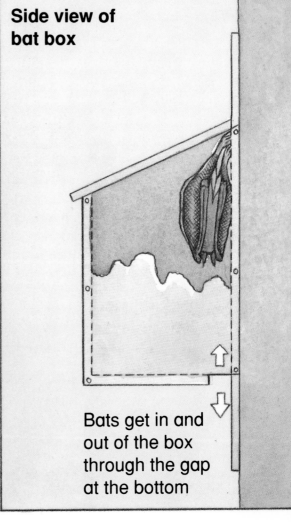

Side view of bat box

Bats get in and out of the box through the gap at the bottom

Hedgehogs

Many hedgehogs are killed on the roads. Hedgehogs nest in warm, dry heaps of leaves or under piles of logs.

A hedgehog nest box

You can help hedgehogs by making a hedgehog nest box. Put some dry grass or hay in a wooden box. Place the box under a large heap of dead leaves and twigs. With luck, a hedgehog will build a nest in the box or sleep in it during the winter.

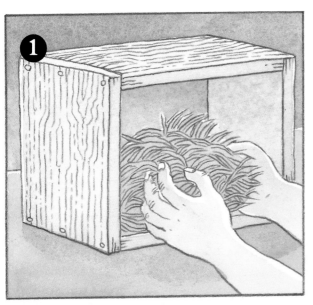

Take care!

Before an adult lights the bonfire, check that a hedgehog is not asleep underneath.

A garden pond

You can make your own mini-pond.

During the spring or summer, dig a hole. Do not make it more than about 30 centimetres deep. Line the hole with a sheet of strong plastic. Tuck the edges down to stop it blowing about. The pictures show you how. Or put a washing-up bowl in a hole in the garden.

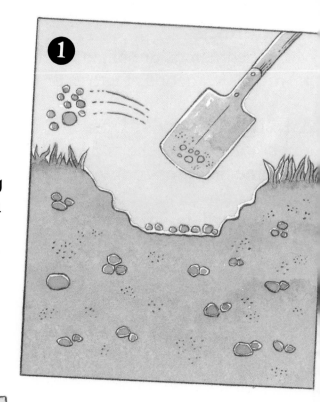

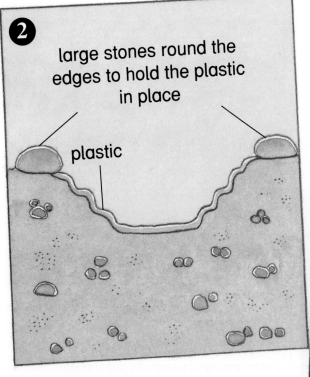

large stones round the edges to hold the plastic in place

plastic

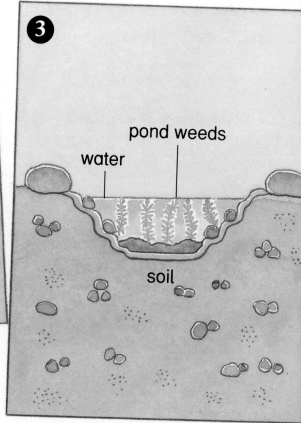

water

pond weeds

soil

Filling your pond

Carefully fill your pond with water. Rainwater is best if you can get some. If you use tap water let it stand for a day or two.

Animals arrive

Watch carefully to see what small animals come to your pond. How do you think they get there? Add some pond weed for them to hide in. If you are lucky you may see a frog or a toad.

Put clean water in your pond if it begins to smell.

More things to do

You saw how to make a bird feeder on page 18.
Here are two more feeders you can make.

Ask an adult to nail some jar
lids to a piece of wood. Put
some bird pudding (see page 19)
or melted fat in each lid. When
the fat is set hard, hang up the
piece of wood.

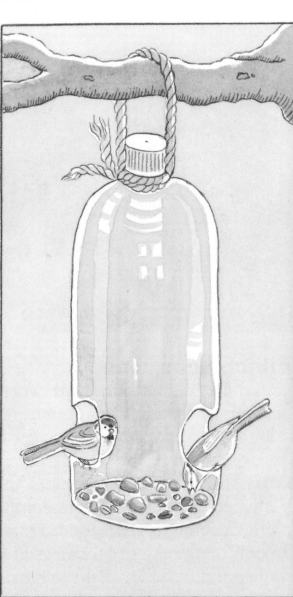

Ask an adult to cut two holes in a
plastic bottle for you. Put breadcrumbs or seeds in it. Hang your
feeder from the branch of a tree.

Glossary

Caterpillar   A long, creeping animal that will turn into a butterfly or moth.

Chemical   A substance used by chemists and in factories. Salt and washing soda are chemicals.

Chrysalis   The form a caterpillar changes into before it becomes a butterfly or moth.

Common   Ordinary, found in many places.

Compost   Rotting leaves and other materials, put on soil to make plants grow better.

Extinct   No longer found. The dinosaur is an extinct animal.

Factory   A building where things are made by machinery.

Insect   A small animal with six legs. Butterflies, bees and flies are insects.

Rare   Not often found. Pandas are rare animals.

Sewage   The waste liquid from a house or town. It is carried away in drains.

Index